THE MYSTERY HEALER

PERRY DANTES

NEWMAN SPRINGS PUBLISHING
320 Broad Street
Red Bank, NJ 07701

First originally published by Newman Springs Publishing 2024

ISBN 979-8-89061-502-2 (Paperback)
ISBN 979-8-89061-503-9 (Digital)

Printed in the United States of America

BETRAYAL

T HE THIRTY-YEAR HISTORY OF THE city of Palo Alto in California, dating from 1960 to 1990, could be best characterized and remembered by the events of the year 1966.

In 1966, Palo Alto, a city south of San Francisco in Santa Clara County, was renowned for its advancements in electronics and computer technology. It was also notable as the location of Stanford University, which was founded in 1885 by Leland Stanford, a prominent railroad official, philanthropist, and former governor of California (1861–1863). Additionally, Stanford served as a member of the US Senate from 1885 to 1893, and he held positions as a financier and director of two major railroads: the Central Pacific and the Southern Pacific.

If the 1960s were characterized by cultural and political turmoil, the residents of Palo Alto in the 1970s shifted their focus to preserving their valuable real estate, channeling their energy toward its protection. Any proposed initiatives or projects faced strong opposition from Palo Alto residents, often resulting in the common response of "Not in my backyard."

During the 1970s, there was a widespread pattern of automatic opposition toward any proposed development. Numerous projects—such as the retirement-housing proposal at St. Patrick's Seminary & University, the DeMonet office towers in East Palo Alto, Menlo Center, the Palo Alto condominium project, and the expansion of the Palo Alto Medical Foundation—faced strong opposition from residents. The primary motivation behind these opposition efforts was the desire to safeguard their quality of life and protect the existing community atmosphere.

The 1980s marked a decade in Palo Alto's history when natural phenomena had a profound impact on the lives of its residents. One notable event occurred in 1985 when a significant fire engulfed homes in the nearby Los Altos Hills area. This disaster was followed by seven years of drought, which heightened concerns about water accessibility not only for Palo Alto but also communities across California. Next, the devastating 1989 Loma Prieta earthquake struck, measuring 6.9 on the Richter scale. This seismic event resulted in extensive damage to various structures including some of Stanford University's older buildings. The cost of repairs alone reached nearly one hundred million dollars.

Why was the year 1966 so unusual, strange, and important? Well, let's examine some key events. On January 12, 1966, Lyndon B. Johnson, the thirty-sixth president of the United States, reaffirmed the country's commitment to remaining in South Vietnam. On January 17, 1966, Martin Luther King Jr. embarked on his civil-rights crusade in Chicago, aiming to address issues such as slums and improve living conditions for Black people. On January 19, 1966, Indira Gandhi assumed office as India's fourth prime minister. Lastly, on January 24, 1966, a tragic incident occurred when an Air India Boeing 707 crashed in Mount Blanc, France, resulting in the loss of 117 lives. This event was a significant tragedy and had a profound impact on so many lives.

On February 10, 1966, Jacqueline Susann's novel *Valley of the Dolls* was published, and it went on to sell an astounding thirty-one million copies. Truly remarkable!

On March 4, 1966, John Lennon of the Beatles made a controversial statement claiming that the Beatles were more popular than Jesus. This remark stirred considerable debate and garnered much attention. Tragically, on March 11, 1966, a devastating fire at a ski resort in Numata, Japan, claimed the lives of thirty-one individuals, marking a profound tragedy. Shifting gears to a more celebratory note, on March 15, 1966, Barbra Streisand and Tom Jones achieved a remarkable feat by winning eight Grammy Awards, a remarkable accomplishment deserving of congratulations. Meanwhile, on March 21, 1966, the number of US soldiers stationed in South Vietnam had reached 215,000, with additional troops arriving daily, reflecting the escalating presence of American forces in the region.

On April 11, 1966, the legendary Frank Sinatra recorded "Strangers in the Night," which went on to become a tremendous hit. On April 13, 1966, Pan Am Airlines placed an order for twenty-five Boeing 747 aircraft, signifying their commitment to serving future customers with these highly sophisticated planes. On April 20, 1966, Bill Russell of the Boston Celtics made history by becoming the first African American coach in NBA history. His achievement was well deserved and significant. On April 30, 1966, the Church of Satan was founded by Anton LaVey in San Francisco, California. This event marked the establishment of a distinctive religious movement, eliciting many diverse opinions.

On June 10, 1966, Janis Joplin held her first concert in San Francisco, marking the beginning of her remarkable musical journey. Bravo, Janis!

On July 1, 1966, Medicare came into effect in the United States, providing health-care coverage for seniors. On July 4, 1966, President Lyndon B. Johnson signed the Freedom of Information Act, a crucial document that aimed to promote transparency and access to information. Its signing was an important milestone.

On August 10, 1966, NASA launched *Lunar Orbiter 1* to the Moon with the purpose of capturing photographs of its surface, contributing to the collective knowledge of humanity.

On August 29, 1966, the Beatles performed their final concert at Candlestick Park in San Francisco, marking the end of an era in their musical journey.

On September 22, 1966, *Surveyor 2* crashed on the Moon during a mission. This event highlighted the challenges and risks involved in lunar exploration. On September 29, 1966, Chevrolet introduced the Camaro, a car that would go on to become immensely popular among young people.

On October 9, 1966, David Cameron was born in London. Little did anyone know at the time that he would later become the

British Prime Minister in 2010. On October 13, 1966, approximately 170 US aircraft bombed North Vietnam as part of an effort to pressure North Vietnamese president Ho Chi Minh into making concessions or ending the war. On October 20, 1966, Jewish writers Shmuel Agnon and Nelly Sachs were awarded the Nobel Prize in Literature. Congratulations for this well-deserved honor!

On October 27, 1966, a poignant photograph emerged from the Vietnam War, featuring a US Marine cradling a small kitten. This touching image captured hearts worldwide, serving as a stark contrast to the harrowing nature of the war. It resonated deeply as an extraordinary symbol of compassion amid the horrors of those times.

On November 8, 1966, Hollywood actor Ronald Reagan was elected as the governor of California, marking a significant milestone in his political career.

On December 15, 1966, the world mourned the loss of Walt Disney, who passed away at the age of sixty-five. Disney was a true genius in the movie industry, leaving an indelible mark on the world of entertainment. On December 28, 1966, a tragic train crash in Everett, Massachusetts, claimed the lives of thirteen people. This event was another devastating tragedy that shook the community.

In summary, 1966 was an unusual and important year marked by significant political events, tragic incidents, and the passing of many notable figures.

In 1966, one of the most beautiful houses in Palo Alto belonged to Dr. Steven Goodman, a renowned surgeon at Stanford University Hospital. Dr. Goodman resided there with his wife Sharon and their nine-year-old daughter, Palmira. Although Dr. Goodman was not particularly fond of the name Palmira, his wife, Sharon, insisted on it because of her love of palm trees. Dr. Goodman cherished Sharon and Palmira. To everyone they encountered, they portrayed the image of an ideal family. Their home was kept in good order by their live-in housekeeper, Paula Niekro.

At the age of thirty-nine, Dr. Goodman was already a talented and young surgeon. During his residency, he initially wanted to specialize in cardiology, but his primary focus shifted to neurosurgery.

His expertise and skills as a surgeon had earned him a reputation across the United States, from New York to California.

In the operating room of Stanford, a group of medical students observed Dr. Goodman through the operating room window as he performed a brain surgery. Every sound that emanated from beneath Dr. Goodman's mask conveyed instructions to his first assistant, Dr. Lawrence Barnes, an African American surgeon. Dr. Barnes flawlessly and promptly followed these instructions, earning Dr. Goodman's unwavering trust and reliance.

From time to time, the second assistant skillfully administered additional general anesthetic containing camphor and atropine for muscle relaxation.

"One more stitch, and the surgery is complete. I'm relieved that we were able to save this patient's life. Let's hope he can endure another six minutes," Dr. Goodman remarked, removing his surgical gloves and blood-spattered coat.

Dr. Barnes enjoyed working alongside Dr. Goodman as their collaborative efforts allowed him to earn a decent income. Their schedules were consistently busy because of Dr. Goodman's reputation as a hardworking physician. He willingly accepted a wide range of surgeries, some of which bordered on the miraculous, much like the procedure he had just performed.

"You're a Jewish genius. A brilliant doctor, Dr. Goodman," Dr. Barnes said.

"Don't exaggerate!" Dr. Goodman replied.

Immediately after the surgery, Dr. Goodman's wife, Sharon, called to remind him not to forget about the concert they had planned to attend at San Francisco's War Memorial Opera House. The renowned Alberto Santini was performing Giacomo Puccini's opera *Turandot*, a show that held special significance for Sharon. She had a deep admiration for Santini's voice and particularly enjoyed the aria "Nessun Dorma."

The performance of "Nessun Dorma" was truly spectacular, captivating the audience. Alberto Santini's rendition was so exceptional that he had to perform it three times as an encore, much to the delight of Dr. Goodman, his wife, and the rest of the enthralled audience. They expressed their appreciation through numerous rounds of applause and standing ovations.

After the performance, Sharon extended an invitation to Alberto Santini and all the artists to their home for a party in honor of the esteemed opera star.

Dr. Barnes, who had joined Dr. and Mrs. Goodman at the opera house, noticed the doctor's uneasiness and inquired, "Did you forget something, Steven?"

"No, it's just that I'm not particularly fond of hosting parties, but I would do anything for my wife," Dr. Goodman replied.

"As always, the parties at your house are enjoyable, with delicious food, great music, and the best company," Dr. Barnes hinted.

Black limousines pulled up in front of the Goodman's property, dropping off the opera performers, who admired Goodman's stunning house.

The party progressed smoothly except for a small hiccup that occurred later and marred the experience. Dr. Goodman noticed Alberto's flirtatious behavior toward his wife. This behavior particularly perturbed Paula. After that, the party atmosphere deteriorated, causing it to end earlier than anticipated.

Two days later, Paula welcomed her friend Maria for their monthly chat at the Goodmans' residence.

"Boy, Sharon Goodman is incredibly fortunate to have such a loving and intelligent husband. Every woman would feel envious," Maria said.

"You're absolutely right. She has everything a woman could dream of. She is beautiful, has a lovely daughter, and is married to a renowned doctor who works tirelessly to provide her with comfort, security, and luxury. I assure you that she appreciates it!" Paula added.

"No doubt about that," Maria replied.

At Stanford University Hospital, Dr. Goodman had just completed another successful brain surgery. This day was not like any other; it marked the Goodmans' ninth wedding anniversary. After the surgery, Dr. Goodman hurriedly made his way to the awaiting limousine and headed home.

But before heading home, he made a quick stop at the jewelry store to purchase an exquisite diamond bracelet as an anniversary gift for Sharon.

As he drove back home, Dr. Goodman found his mind bombarded with thoughts about his wife. The incident at the party where she had flirted with Alberto Santini triggered a flurry of memories from their nine years of marriage. While he knew Sharon admired Santini's voice, he couldn't help but wonder if her admiration had crossed the line into something deeper. Could she be falling in love with him? No. He dismissed the thought, assuring himself that it was impossible.

Dr. Goodman was deeply in love with his wife and recognized that their ways of expressing affection differed. Sharon was delicate, always wearing a smile, but he couldn't shake the feeling that she didn't reciprocate his love in the same way. He reminded himself that he owed his success to her unwavering support and attributed his accomplishments to her presence in his life. To sort through his thoughts, he asked his driver to slow down, giving himself more time to reflect on their nine years together. He realized that their marriage had been devoid of arguments and mistrust, yet he felt as though he were the only one who openly shared his thoughts, fears, and emotions. Sharon, on the other hand, seemed guarded, perhaps unsure of how to express her own feelings.

Although the limo's pace had slowed, they eventually arrived at Dr. Goodman's house. Stepping out of the vehicle with the diamond bracelet in hand, ready to surprise Sharon, he noticed his housekeeper, Paula, standing in front of the house, her tear-streaked face catching his attention.

"What happened? Where is Sharon?" he inquired, his voice filled with concern.

At first, Paula said nothing, but then she burst into a fresh flood of tears.

"Where is Sharon? What happened?" Dr. Goodman asked again. A sense of impending doom gripped his heart.

Dr. Goodman entered the house and immediately noticed a letter lying on the table. He picked it up and started to read.

My dear Steven!

I don't know if you will ever be able to for-
give me, but I am leaving you.

The words began to whirl in front of his eyes. Beads of sweat
covered his forehead, and for a moment, he stopped breathing.

"Where is she?" he asked, his voice choked with sobs.

"Sharon left with Palmira," Paula said quietly.

"You're lying! That's not true!" Dr. Goodman said nervously.

"I called a taxi for her. She only took two pieces of luggage,"
Paula added.

Dr. Goodman went to his study and continued to read Sharon's
letter.

I fell in love with Alberto Santini. It happened so fast; he swept me off my feet. I am a
weak woman. I know today is our wedding anniversary, and you probably bought me something
special, which I can't accept now.

Dr. Goodman stared at the diamond bracelet he took out of his
pocket and continued reading Sharon's letter.

Steven, I never loved you enough. I don't
think I'm worthy of you. I can't bear the thought
of your fame, your wealth, and my own insignif-
icance beside you. I am taking Palmira with me.
I was always faithful to you, but I can't continue
any longer. Goodbye, Steven.

Sharon

Dr. Goodman replayed Sharon's words in his mind: "I never
loved you. I was tired of your wealth, your fame, and my insignifi-
cance next to you."

"Why, Sharon?" he kept asking himself, trying to comprehend her decision. However, he found it impossible to understand. These thoughts echoed in his mind: *She left. She took Palmira. She loves Alberto Santini.* It seemed unimaginable to him.

Suddenly there was a knock at the door.

"Is it her? Has she come back?" Dr. Goodman exclaimed.

"Hello," a deep voice greeted him. It was his brother, Joshua Goodman. Joshua was a lawyer working for the Army. He looked around but couldn't spot Sharon with his brother, sensing that something was amiss.

"Where is Sharon?" Joshua inquired.

"She left. She went abroad. She took Palmira with her. It happened today," Dr. Goodman replied.

"Today?" Joshua questioned, visibly puzzled.

"Yes, I sent her there. There were certain matters to attend to," he explained, his voice strained, bearing the burden of suffering etched on his face.

"I understand, but what about the invitations to your anniversary party? Should I call everyone and cancel?" Joshua asked.

"Go ahead," Dr. Goodman responded.

"I'll get a list from Paula. Could you do me a favor, Steve, and get some rest? You look very tired. Goodbye for now," Josh said as he left. Joshua's advice sounded good, but taking a nap was the last thing Steven could think about.

"I think I need a drink," he said, putting on his jacket.

"Are you leaving, Doctor?" Paula asked.

"Yes, I just want to take a walk to clear my head. I need some fresh air."

There was a nice restaurant nearby called Ram's Head Inn that he was heading to, but the only thing he could think about was Sharon.

"How could she do it?" he asked himself.

She left so suddenly, leaving a man like him, who would do anything to keep her happy. Did he do anything to hurt her? It never crossed his mind that 1966 would be such an unpredictable year.

He muttered to himself as he walked. Passersby watched him with concern, but he looked like he didn't care about anything. He had never visited Ram's Head Inn. But the only thing on his mind was to have a drink, and this was the closest place he could find.

He walked into the restaurant, went straight to the bar, and ordered a shot of whiskey. The first sip of whiskey brought him some relief, warming his throat and stomach.

There were three men sitting at a nearby table, talking loudly and using foul language. It didn't bother him, and after he had another sip of whiskey, he bought a bottle and placed it on their table. He felt like he needed some company to have another drink.

"Let's have a drink, guys," he said, inviting the three men.

The shorter man introduced himself as Frank. The second guy, tall and skinny, named Jack, said that he loved whiskey and would be happy to join him, thanking Dr. Goodman for his generosity. The third man, Bill, called fatso by the other two, grabbed the bottle and poured the whiskey into four glasses. Dr. Goodman ordered another bottle of whiskey. Jack noticed something was off about Dr. Goodman and started asking him a few questions.

"Did you go bankrupt? Did you lose your job?" he asked.

Dr. Goodman lowered his head and said, "My wife left me."

"So what?" Jack asked.

"She was everything to me," he replied.

Dr. Goodman had another drink and shuddered. For the first time in his life, he hated the taste of alcohol. It went straight to his head, and he started feeling woozy.

Dr. Goodman paid the bartender for the two bottles with a crisp hundred-dollar bill from his pocket. His three drinking companions assumed he had more money on him. Big-bellied Bill ordered Frank to get his car. He told the bartender that they knew where Dr. Goodman lived and would get him home safely.

Jack, Bill, and Frank held Dr. Goodman up as he staggered to the car. They helped Dr. Goodman into the back seat of Frank's car and started driving toward San Jose. Bill searched Dr. Goodman's pockets, found his wallet, took all the money, and threw the wallet out of the window. He also discovered the diamond bracelet in one of Dr. Goodman's pockets and exclaimed while showing it to the others, "Guys, look what I found! It seems like we hit the jackpot."

"Let's dump him now that he's useless to us," Frank ordered.

On hearing this, Dr. Goodman regained consciousness and screamed, "WHAT ARE YOU DOING?"

Bill opened the door and pushed Dr. Goodman out of the car, which was traveling over forty miles per hour. His seemingly weightless body hit the ground. The three thugs continued driving toward San Jose, leaving Dr. Goodman for dead.

Meanwhile, after performing in Chicago, Boston, and New York, Alberto Santini returned to Rome together with Sharon and her daughter, Palmira. They stayed in his apartment, and he even found an English school for Palmira so she could continue her studies.

JOHN DOE

Dr. Goodman's lifeless and battered body lay sprawled on the side of the road. He had been callously thrown out of a speeding car by a gang of thugs who robbed and left him for dead. It was a tragic sight—a man of his stature first humiliated by his wife and now left unconscious and discarded on the roadside. Dr. Goodman's vast knowledge and exceptional talent in the field of medicine had earned him a well-deserved reputation as a surgical expert, but now his fate hung in the balance.

Fortunately, fate intervened when Hector Morales, a compassionate Latino man from San Jose, happened to drive by in his pickup truck. Hector and his son Julio were returning from a supply run to San Francisco for their family business, Morales Bakery. When they noticed Dr. Goodman's injured body, they immediately stopped the truck to help.

"Dad, this man is badly hurt, but he's still breathing! He's alive! We must do something," Julio pleaded with his father.

"Are you from Frisco?" Hector asked Dr. Goodman.

"I…I don't know," came a weak whisper.

With utmost care, Hector and Julio lifted Dr. Goodman and gently placed him in the back of their pickup truck.

"We must rush him to the hospital in San Jose," Hector declared, a sense of urgency in his voice.

After a long and stressful drive, they arrived at San Jose's Good Samaritan Hospital. The ER doctors and nurses quickly attended to Dr. Goodman while Hector answered their questions about the man he brought to the hospital. Unfortunately, they found no wallet or identification on him. The hospital authorities promptly notified the San Jose Police Department, urging them to search for any missing persons in the area matching Dr. Goodman's description.

Meanwhile, in Palo Alto, Dr. Goodman's housekeeper, Paula, had already alerted the San Francisco police and the local newspaper, the *San Francisco Sentinel*, about his disappearance. He seemed to have vanished without a trace.

The ER doctor informed Hector that the unidentified patient would be kept at the hospital overnight for further observation to ensure there were no hidden injuries. The doctor asked Hector to return the next morning for an update on the patient's condition.

The following day, filled with hope, Hector and Julio returned to the hospital, eager to learn if the man's identity had been discovered. However, they received disappointing news: it remained a mystery.

"Doctor, perhaps we should refer to him as John Doe," suggested Julio, pointing toward the unconscious man.

"Very well. Let's call him John Doe. Aside from the visible injuries, like scratches, cuts, and bruises, John Doe is facing a more significant challenge. He has lost his memory, most likely due to the trauma of hitting his head on the pavement after being thrown out of a car. It's a serious condition that requires immediate attention," the ER doctor explained.

"This is devastating news. We'll continue trying to locate his family," Hector replied with determination.

The doctor prepared discharge papers for Hector to sign, officially transferring the responsibility of John Doe's care to him. The doctor assured Hector that they would continue their efforts to uncover any information about John Doe's identity.

"Doctor, I believe I can offer this man a job in my bakery. He appears to be strong and capable," Hector proposed.

"Before proceeding, I recommend seeking legal advice regarding John Doe's situation," the doctor advised. "After all, you found him, and he owes his life to you and your son. He has survived a terrible ordeal."

With the paperwork completed, Hector, Julio, and John Doe left the hospital. As they drove toward Hector's home, they continued questioning the stranger.

"Do you remember anything now? Your name, perhaps?" Hector gently inquired.

"What…what is my name? No…I don't know. I don't remember," John Doe replied slowly and with frustration.

"It seems the doctor was right. He has no recollection. His memory is lost," Hector confided in Julio. "For simplicity's sake, let's give him a proper name for when we introduce him to our family. How about Juan Alvarez?"

On reaching the Morales' family bakery, Hector introduced Juan to his wife Dolores and his younger son, Ruben. He explained the entire situation, sharing how they could support Juan in adapting to his new circumstances. Hector also discovered a means of obtaining a Social Security card for Juan's employment through a man named Antonio Diaz. The next day, Hector met Diaz, paid him five hundred dollars for the documentation, and procured a Social Security card for Juan. Hector hired Juan Alvarez in his bakery, offering him minimum wage for his labor.

On Juan's first day, Hector pulled Julio aside and said, "Aren't we fortunate to have Juan working with us? He's a strong man, and we could use his help. Let's try to be patient with him as he recovers from this accident. Teach him the art of preparing the dough for churros, empanadas, and conchas. He seems smart, so I'm sure he'll learn quickly." As the months passed, Hector grew exceedingly pleased with Juan's dedicated work ethic.

Meanwhile, Dr. Goodman's mysterious disappearance continued to weigh heavily on the city of Palo Alto. The uncertainty surrounding his fate stirred curiosity and concern among its residents. Those who knew him well found the idea of suicide inconceivable. Dr. Goodman had a deep love for his work, his family, and life itself. He exuded a passionate vitality that set him apart as a doctor, earning him the admiration of both colleagues and patients.

The possibility of murder was also deemed unlikely. How could such a revered and respected surgeon have enemies? He was a vital asset to the community. If his demise had been the result of a random act of violence, his lifeless body surely would have been discovered. What caused him to lose his memory? A year earlier, in 1965, local police found ten seemingly healthy individuals wandering around Palo Alto, suffering from memory loss.

Dr. Goodman's brother, Joshua, took matters into his own hands, summoning the local police captain to discuss his brother's disappearance. As the captain searched Goodman's residence, he made a startling discovery—a loaded gun.

"It seems unlikely that my brother committed suicide, considering his gun is still here," Joshua informed the captain.

"While the evidence might not point to the possibility of suicide, I haven't entirely ruled out the notion of foul play, perhaps an accidental death. In that case, I will distribute Dr. Goodman's photograph to all police stations," declared the captain, determined to unravel the truth.

DR. JUAN

I T WAS 1970. FOUR YEARS had passed since Dr. Goodman's disappearance. Juan Alvarez enjoyed working at Hector Morales's bakery, but not remembering anything from his past was troubling him. Subconsciously he sensed that something was missing.

One day, while working at the bakery, Julio complained about some pain in his right arm.

"Let me see it," Juan offered. He examined Julio's arm and noticed that something was wrong. "Did you break your arm in the past?" he asked.

"Yes, a couple of years ago while playing baseball," Julio replied.

Juan carefully examined it further and asked, "Who treated you when you broke it?"

"Some doctor at San Jose's Good Samaritan Hospital. It still bothers me," Julio explained.

"Do you remember the name of that doctor?" Juan inquired.

"I think his name was Dr. Fernando Sanchez. He still works at our local Latino clinic," Julio answered.

"Let's go see him," Juan suggested.

Dr. Sanchez's clinic was a few blocks away from the bakery. Juan, Julio, and Hector walked to the clinic; and after a short wait, they were able to see Dr. Sanchez.

"Good day, gentlemen. How can I assist you?" Dr. Sanchez greeted them, recognizing Hector and Julio.

"Sorry, Doctor, but you might have to help this young man again. The bones in his right arm didn't heal properly. Do you remember him?" Juan pointed at Julio.

"Yes, I do. Can I ask how you know him?" Dr. Sanchez asked.

Juan remained silent, so Hector interjected. "This is Juan. He works in my bakery, but we call him Dr. Juan because he's already helped one of my workers who got injured on the job."

"Dr. Juan? Interesting," Fernando Sanchez remarked. Dr. Sanchez acknowledged that Julio's arm hadn't healed properly, so he scheduled Julio for corrective surgery.

The next day, Hector informed his family that Juan would now be known as Dr. Juan. Although Juan still had no memory of his past, something about being called Dr. Juan resonated with him. Hector, pleased with Dr. Juan's medical expertise, even put up a sign in front of the bakery stating that anyone seeking medical advice should ask for Juan.

Word quickly spread among San Jose's Latino community about Dr. Juan. Some bakery clients began approaching Dr. Juan with various medical questions. Soon Dr. Juan found himself assisting more and more people who trusted his medical knowledge. They could have gone to the local clinic, but they felt more comfortable seeking advice from Dr. Juan.

However, there were limits to what he could do. One woman brought her eleven-year-old daughter with a cleft lip, begging for his help. In normal circumstances, he would have been able to assist; but without his memory and lacking the necessary instruments, he advised the distraught mother to visit the clinic and find a doctor who could provide the required care. Unfortunately, examining this girl didn't help trigger any memories of his own daughter, Palmira.

People continued to seek Dr. Juan's help with broken arms, broken legs, and other orthopedic problems, and he did his best to assist them. One day, Camille, Dolores's sister, was at the bakery, talking to Dr. Juan about some of her latest health issues, and he diagnosed her with experiencing recurrent episodes of epilepsy. Concerned for her well-being, he began researching medicinal herbs and their uses for treating various ailments. He contemplated exploring local forests to search for different herbs that could potentially help Camille.

The following day, Hector drove Dr. Juan to a woodland area near San Jose. After providing him with directions on how to return to the bakery, Hector left him there. Dr. Juan spent several hours walking through the forest, gathering different herbs. However, he couldn't find his way back to the bakery after he returned to San Jose. A policeman noticed him aimlessly wandering the streets and approached him.

"What are you doing here? Are you lost? Do you have any identification, like a driver's license?" the policeman inquired.

"No, I don't have any. I was looking for and gathering some herbal plants," Dr. Juan replied.

"And what is your name?" the policeman asked.

"I don't know. I don't remember," he replied.

Dr. Juan couldn't comprehend why the policeman was regarding him with suspicion, as if he were a common criminal. It seemed that having proper identification and remembering his name were important things he should know. Suddenly he felt the need to run but was unaware of which direction. His anxiety took over, and he felt caught in a whirlwind. Helpless and disoriented, he clung to his consciousness. The policeman interrupted him.

"Where do you live?" the policeman asked.

"I work at Morales Bakery, and I live there as well," Dr. Juan replied.

The policeman knew where the bakery was and offered him a ride home. Dr. Juan felt relieved that the ordeal had come to an end, grateful to be back in a familiar place. He thanked the policeman for the ride and hurried back to the bakery to share his experience with everyone.

Dr. Juan took all the herbs he had gathered to his room and contemplated which ones could be used to heal. So far he planned to use herbs to treat common ailments, such as colds and stomach problems. However, for more-serious health issues, he would still urge his patients to visit a doctor.

He used chamomile tea to treat stomach pains; valerian drops to calm nerves; mint for chest pains; and American linden for heartburn, anxiety, and sore throat. Dr. Juan provided an alkaloid ergot (bot. *Claviceps purpurea*) to a woman suffering from migraines; and a few days later, she returned, overwhelmed with gratitude as her headaches had completely disappeared. Another woman complained of liver issues whenever she ate something disagreeable. Dr. Juan gave her some wormwood herb, assuring her that it should help.

There was a frightening incident once when a man came to see Dr. Juan, complaining of abdominal pain, nausea, and tingling in his fingers and toes. Hector remembered this man was cheating on his wife with a younger woman. He suspected that his jealous wife might be attempting to poison him. Dr. Juan considered the possibility of arsenic poisoning and urgently requested Hector to call 911 for an ambulance. The man was fortunate to have sought Dr. Juan's help as his intervention potentially averted a tragic outcome. The incident was later investigated by the police as an attempted murder by the man's wife.

One day, Hector Morales called Dr. Juan into his private room and presented him with a large piece of gold.

"My grandfather, who was a Hopi Indian, gave this to me before he died. Take it," Hector said, offering the gold piece to Dr. Juan.

Dr. Juan was taken aback and declined the gift. "I appreciate the gesture, but I cannot accept it. I don't need any more money, especially gold. I'm content with what I earn from my work," Dr. Juan replied. He also never accepted any money from his patients despite their attempts to compensate him. He derived happiness from helping those who needed his assistance.

Years had passed, and the disappearance of Dr. Steven Goodman was gradually forgotten. Dr. Lawrence Barnes, Goodman's assistant at Stanford University Hospital, was promoted to head of the department. With his exceptional surgical skills, he became a renowned specialist.

It was no surprise when a biographical book titled *Dr. Steven Goodman: A Genial Surgeon* appeared in bookstores. The book, authored by Dr. Lawrence Barnes, chronicled all of Dr. Goodman's accomplishments and ended with this final sentence: "To pay tribute to the late Dr. Steven Goodman, a good man and the finest surgeon, the American medical community mourns his tragic disappearance, which seems destined to remain shrouded in mystery."

And so the story of Dr. Steven Goodman concluded, his memory preserved through Dr. Lawrence Barnes's moving tribute. Dr. Juan, despite his amnesia, continued providing medical guidance and assistance to the Latino community in San Jose, gaining even more trust and admiration. He found purpose in his role as Dr. Juan, using his knowledge of herbs and remedies to alleviate the ailments of those who sought his help. Although his past remained elusive, Dr. Juan embraced his newfound identity and fulfilled his calling to serve others.

SZYMON TYMOR AND PALMIRA GOODMAN

Szymon Tymor was born in Poland in 1951, six years after the end of World War II. He was born in the city of Torun, located about two hundred kilometers north of Warsaw, the capital of Poland. Torun was the birthplace of the famous astronomer Nicolaus Copernicus (Mikołaj Kopernik in Polish). He developed the Copernican system, or theory, that the sun is the center of the solar system and that all planets, including Earth, orbit around it.

In 1966, Szymon emigrated with his parents to the United States. It was always their dream to live in the beautiful state of California. Szymon, fifteen years old, was enrolled at Lowell High School in San Francisco.

Szymon was a very handsome boy with a slender posture, a dark complexion, and very large brown eyes. His eyes were his most attractive and charming feature.

From his first day at Lowell High School, Szymon made many friends. Mark Meihsner became his best friend. Both were into sports, especially football and tennis. They had a very good sense of humor, could laugh at each other's jokes, and never held any grudges.

After they both graduated high school in 1970, they attended Stanford University. Szymon graduated in 1974 with a major in journalism, and he quickly found a job in his field at the *San Francisco Sentinel.* He enjoyed working there and liked his colleagues, especially his boss, Pat Greenland.

In the meantime, Mark graduated from law school in June 1977. Szymon was invited to his graduation party and met a girl there named Cheryl Walker. They started talking, and when she learned he was born in Poland, she wanted to learn more about the exotic foreign country he came from.

Mark was serving drinks. Cheryl ordered a Manhattan and was not surprised when Szymon asked for vodka gimlet.

"Now I know where you learned to drink vodka." Cheryl laughed.

"My father used to say that vodka is the purest alcohol on the market," Szymon replied.

"It's possible! So tell me more about yourself," she said, continuing the conversation.

"I came to the United States when I was fifteen years old. I was brought up Catholic, which was my father's influence, but I must admit that both of my parents were not very religious," Szymon said.

"Tell me more about your parents," she asked.

"Okay. My father, Edmund, was a historian and philosopher at the University of Torun. When he came here to the United States, it was very hard for him to adjust to life in a new country. Without perfect knowledge of the English language, he couldn't work in his profession, which he loved dearly. He started considering himself useless to society," Szymon explained.

"Why?" she asked.

"Well, when he got a teaching position at the local community college, he tried incorporating his knowledge of history and philosophy into the classroom. But the students were more interested in playing football, basketball, or baseball rather than discussing the German philosopher Immanuel Kant* or composers like Frédéric Chopin* or Felix Mendelssohn.* He often made comparisons between the turbulent histories of the United States and Poland, finding similarities in fighting for freedom and democracy," Szymon said.

"Continue please," Cheryl asked.

"My father was born in the city of Plock*, located near Warsaw. It's situated on the Vistula River, the longest river in Poland, and flows from the south to the Baltic Sea*," he continued.

"Tell me more," Cheryl insisted.

"When I was young, my father told me stories about him and his younger brother, Casimir. They used to swim in the Vistula, but there was a very dangerous vortex in the river that could drag swimmers to the bottom and cause them to drown. Some of the best swimmers lost their lives. Every time my father and his brother went swimming, my grandmother worried sick about them. One day, Casimir was swimming too closely behind a barge in the river. He was so close he could've been pulled in by its propellers. The shaft's blades would've cut him to pieces if my father wasn't so quick in thinking. He pulled him from danger and saved his brother's life, making him an instant hero in the city. My father was a proud and gentle man. He loved his life in California but had heart problems and died of a heart attack a couple years ago," Szymon ended.

"And your mother?" Cheryl asked.

"My mother, Sabina, is Jewish, so I'm half Jewish. In our home, Jewishness was difficult to define. My mother recognized herself as a secular Jew. She is a beautiful, educated, and energetic woman. She is very strong-minded but also has a soft side. She loves poetry and often quoted the Persians who said that 'good poets are like angels of heaven' and fellow Poles who said that 'a poet was born a hundred years before the beginning of the earth.' I think I acquired a natural aptitude for poetry from my mother," Szymon said.

"Have you written any poetry?" Cheryl asked.

"I wrote one poem when I was very young," he replied.

"And what happened to it?" Cheryl insisted.

"It was published in the *San Francisco Sentinel,*" he replied.

"You see, someone appreciated your talent! What was its title?" she asked.

"'The Wanderer Goes Home,'" Szymon replied.

"What was it about?" she urged.

"It was about the Jewish people making their final return to Israel after an eternal diaspora," Szymon answered.

"It must have been interesting," she said.

"I'm also into some trifle stories and proverbs," Szymon added.

"Can you recite some funny poems of yours?" Cheryl asked.

"I wrote one poem for my father titled 'The Search,' and it goes like this." Szymon started to recite his poem.

> The searchers are looking for a light
> Into the German Fahrenheit's childhood.
> Who was really that Fahrenheit?
> They have to change their mood.
> Reaumur was French, Celsius a Swede.
> Their discoveries dazzled.
> So how does this German get into scale?
> This Fahrenheit? A real puzzle.
> So many suppositions hatched,
> Some very old and some new.
> Was he a German or a Dutch?
> Maybe a Greek or a Jew?
> But for me, one thing is clear
> He couldn't be a Russian or Pole
> For they could invent anything without fear
> But never a thermometer of alcohol.
> Why pour vodka into a tube?
> Isn't it wasteful? I'd like to take a vote.
> Isn't it better and healthier
> To pour it down your throat?

Cheryl started laughing and couldn't stop.
"Did you like it?" he asked.
"Tell me another one," Cheryl asked politely.
"Okay. Here is one about an illiterate girl."

> She looked lovely and charming, so I took a bait,
> She was very beautiful but illiterate.
> And now, when I think of her less and less,
> I see her a.. in my mind, written with only one *S*.

Cheryl laughed loudly.

Szymon continued sharing more quips with her. "How about these two about male weakness? 'You have to be a strong male if your weakness is a female' or 'Before he is going steady, he thinks of the bed already.'"

In June 1975, Szymon and Cheryl started dating. They were always so happy in each other's company. When they had been dating for six months, Cheryl invited Szymon and his best friend, Mark Meihsner, to a New Year's Eve party she was having at her house.

First, they met at Someplace Else, a restaurant where only the most important people of San Francisco dined. While walking to the meeting place, Szymon looked around and admired the city's class and sophistication.

Someplace Else was located inside the Hilton hotel. Szymon had to push through the crowd to find Mark and Cheryl. They found an empty table and ordered some drinks. Of course, Szymon ordered his favorite, the vodka gimlet.

"Szymon, I must admit some of your articles in the *Sentinel* are quite controversial. Aren't you afraid that you're being too straightforward?" Mark asked.

"Not really because truth is the only way to deal with anything," Szymon replied calmly.

"We must get together soon for a game of tennis. It's been a long time since we played," Mark said, trying to change the subject.

"I still remember a birthday card from you wishing me at least one defeat in our countless matches," Szymon said, laughing.

"Yes, those were great times, although I was getting tired of always losing to you," Mark commented.

Cheryl noticed a woman sitting at the next table. She was sure she knew her. "Do you see that woman in the white jumper suit?" she asked.

"Yes, what's so special about her?" Szymon inquired.

"I heard she just got married for the third time to some French man. His name is Pierre Loreant, if I'm not mistaken. My friend handled her last divorce. Her last husband left her loads of money," Cheryl said.

"I believe it. Women have their own ways," Szymon replied and then started reciting,

> Her first husband was Bob, the second John
> Now she's got Pierre for today
> When someone finds a faithful wife,
> They all would like to marry her

"You and your poetry," Cheryl said with a short laugh.

After having two more drinks and discussing their jobs, they were ready to head to Cheryl's New Year's Eve party. While they waited for the valet to bring Mark his car, they continued with some small talk.

"Do I look nice enough?" Cheryl asked, straightening up her hair.

"You look terrific," Mark complimented her.

"I hope you'll like my parents," Cheryl said.

After driving for thirty minutes, they reached Cheryl's home in the Presidio area of San Francisco. During their drive, Cheryl talked about her influential family. Szymon was hardly listening, but Mark was impressed.

"We're almost here. Turn left into the next driveway," Cheryl said.

Looking around at the area homes, Szymon and Mark realized that this must be the nicest neighborhood in San Francisco. Before they entered the house, Cheryl whispered something to Szymon.

"Please don't mention anything about you being half Jewish."

"Why? Are you ashamed of me?" Szymon asked, disappointed. He was never one to hide his feelings.

If he knew that he wouldn't feel welcome in Cheryl's house, he would have turned down her invitation to the party. However, his quick wit and poetic sensibility came to the rescue, defusing the tension and saving the situation. He looked around and started to recite a poem.

> I know you look for glory, fame with your aristo-
> cratic name,

> Perhaps you've got a Jewish soul, though you are
> > Italian,
> French, or Pole,
> For if you followed your history through,
> You'd find your grandad was a Jew!

"You and your poetry again," said Mark with a big smile.

Cheryl looked astonished, not knowing what to say. When they walked inside, they were greeted warmly by the Walkers. Szymon liked Cheryl's mother from the start. He felt very comfortable in the company of this elegant gray-haired lady. She seemed to like Szymon too. She appreciated his charm and good looks. When Szymon kissed her hand, which was a common way to greet a lady in Poland, she was even more charmed by him. She liked Mark too, but there was something special about Szymon.

Cheryl's dad, Mr. John Walker, didn't make a good first impression on Szymon. Szymon already felt a little premature bias toward him after overhearing a conversation at the office that John Walker was dishonest and made money off welfare cases. John Walker was a short, heavyset man with beady eyes.

Szymon looked around at all the guests. He assumed many of them were members of the Walker family. Some were pleasant, and some were not, just like in any other family. He was a little disappointed because he was expecting more entertainment at this party. After all, it was New Year's Eve! Instead, he just felt bored.

"Cheryl told us you're a journalist, Mr. Tymor. Which newspaper do you work for?" asked a curious John Walker.

"The *San Francisco Sentinel*," Szymon answered.

"It must be an exciting job with all the turmoil going on in the world today. Isn't it also dangerous?" he asked.

"Yes, somewhat," Szymon replied.

Szymon realized that the only thing Mr. Walker knew about and was interested in was how to make money. He was not interested in Szymon's job; it might be noble to write about the world's problems, but it didn't bring you money.

If your business is honey, you will always find an opportunity to lick it crossed Szymon's mind.

John Walker lived in an affluent and predominantly White neighborhood and loved indulging in his daily ritual of savoring a scotch on the rocks, blissfully unconcerned with the plight of Black Americans, Latinos, or other minorities in San Francisco. The thought of Polish or Jewish Americans never even crossed his mind. Raising his glass of scotch, he proclaimed, "Cheers to our guests, to our health, and to the new year. Welcome, 1977!"

Szymon, joining in the toast and enthusiastically added, "*Na zdrowie! L'chaim!*"

Mr. Walker's expression turned sour after Szymon's toast. A thought crossed Szymon's mind: *There is a saying that the bitter taste of the world is disliked mostly by those who never reached a tasting shop.* Although Szymon felt slightly offended by Mr. Walker's reaction to learning about his Jewish heritage, he attributed it to Mr. Walker's inebriation.

Feeling momentarily like an outcast among the seemingly carefree partygoers, Szymon sought solace in another drink and approached John Walker once more.

"You know, Mr. Walker, even though I'm Catholic and was raised in a Christian manner, I learned Polish from my father and Yiddish from my mother," Szymon explained.

"I always told Cheryl that it never hurts to learn an additional language. She knows a bit of Spanish," replied John Walker.

"Very good. Every bit helps in life," Szymon acknowledged. "Look, Mr. Walker, if you're interested in learning more about Jews, I'd be happy to share what I've learned over the years. The nation of Israel has been reborn, ready to fight for their land to the death. The Jewish people were educated and skilled in their trades but only earned the respect of others when they learned how to defend them-selves. Isn't it ironic? Don't you think? I hope this resilient nation lives on forever. Eretz Israel!" Szymon concluded.

The entire gathering erupted in applause, congratulating Szymon on his speech. It wasn't just the speech itself; Szymon's personal charm added a special touch to the entire incident. Cheryl approached Szymon and planted a kiss on his cheek.

Szymon couldn't help but envy Cheryl's privileged upbringing and affluent lifestyle. Her family had wealth, allowing her to travel extensively and study at prestigious European universities in Paris and London. While she might not have been the most diligent student, it hardly mattered as her father could afford to support her every desire.

"You're quite fortunate that your father has money," Szymon remarked.

"Having money isn't as bad as not having it." Cheryl laughed at own clever comment.

"If she continues to behave like a child at the age of twenty-one, she'll remain shallow for the rest of her life," Szymon quietly whispered to himself.

"What did you say?" Cheryl inquired after overhearing Szymon's whisper.

"Nothing important," Szymon replied, brushing it off.

Cheryl, already a bit tipsy from a few drinks, appeared somewhat melancholic.

"Don't be sad, Cheryl. Let me try to lift your spirits with a bit of my poetry. Listen carefully." Szymon began reciting,

> Me? I'd like to be somebody I'm not.
> I talk about nothing a lot.
> But when I have to take something from blind
>   or deaf,
> I'd rather give away something I don't have.

Uncertain whether to laugh, Cheryl shrugged it off, not fully grasping the meaning. Szymon quickly switched gears, reciting another one of his short poems.

> I got a patent for my new discovery, for losses or
>   gains,
> I shortened the path to some people's brains.

As Szymon concluded, Cheryl let out a forced laugh. Just then, John Walker approached and pulled Szymon aside by the elbow.

"You know, Mr. Tymor, your speech about Jewish people was quite impressive. Have you ever considered becoming a lawyer?" Walker asked.

"Oh, no. That's my best friend Mark's area of expertise. Law is his domain," Szymon replied, gesturing toward Mark.

"Are you sure?" Walker inquired.

"Yes, I'm a journalist, and I love my job," Szymon reaffirmed.

"Well, then let's drink to that and the new year. Let's hope it brings us all good news," Walker cheered.

"Forget about politics, race, and religion!" Cheryl exclaimed, running around in a slightly drunken state after consuming several glasses of champagne.

Everyone was joyful and tipsy except Szymon. Cheryl approached him and whispered, "What are you thinking about, Szymon?"

"Happiness. How to achieve genuine happiness," Szymon replied.

"Well, so far I haven't found anyone who can make me happy," Cheryl confessed.

Szymon was taken back by this comment but not surprised, considering what he had heard about Cheryl and her promiscuous life as a student.

"I always felt adept in this realm. I've known many men, but they were all so easy to forget about. Every man seemed different, yet all were essentially the same. After just a few minutes, I could classify them into distinct categories. The first type was easy to talk to and just as easy to manage. When they laid their heads on the pillow, I could do anything I wanted. Their demands were modest. The second type was tougher, requiring steel nerves and strength. This type didn't know how to respect women. They treated us like machines ready for anything. I disliked men who rambled on about their past. They were usually dull, searching for a mother figure in every woman they met. I've encountered many great men, those who appreciated the beauty of art or were confident enough to think they could change the world overnight. However, there was one courageous man who proposed to me, but I wasn't ready for that level of commitment," Cheryl divulged.

Szymon and Mark were somewhat surprised by Cheryl's candidness about her experiences with men.

As the party ended, Szymon and Mark left the Walker residence, and Szymon whispered, "You see, Mark, if a Jewish man is sweet, people want to embrace him with delight. But if he turns bitter, they prefer to spit him out."

In September 1977, Szymon Tymor's boss, Pat Greenland, called him into his office. As Szymon entered, Pat gestured toward the chair across from him.

"Please have a seat, Szymon. You're my finest journalist. Let me begin with what I have to say. Last month, Alex Haley's bestseller *Roots* became a sensation in the market, captivating readers searching for their heritage. Notably, there has been a 50 percent increase in passengers traveling from the United States to Poland, mostly Polish Americans. People of various origins, proud of their heritage, have begun visiting their respective ancestral countries," Pat Greenland explained.

"In that case, would you like me to go to Poland? Perhaps I could trace some of my relatives. I have a cousin, an architect, who lives near Warsaw," Szymon suggested.

"Slow down. Not so fast. I don't want you to go to Poland just yet. Your next assignment will take you to Rome, Italy," Pat revealed.

"*Really?*" Szymon exclaimed, surprised by the unexpected opportunity.

"Listen carefully. You were only fifteen in 1966, so you probably don't remember an incident in Palo Alto involving the famous surgeon Steven Goodman and his wife, Sharon, who fell in love with the renowned opera singer Alberto Santini. Most people have long forgotten about the mysterious disappearance of Dr. Steven Goodman. At the time, his daughter, Palmira, was only nine years old. Now, at nineteen, she's planning to attend Stanford University this fall. I want you to go to Rome and interview her," Pat Greenland explained.

"Are you certain she's in Rome?" Szymon inquired.

"Sharon Goodman and Palmira followed Alberto Santini to Rome. From what I know, Palmira loved her father very much, so I assume she still misses him terribly and wants to find out what happened. The whole incident surrounding her father was incredibly sad and tragic. I heard that Palmira still attends the American Overseas School of Rome since Alberto wanted her going to the best school in Rome. So, Szymon, good luck, and bon voyage!" Pat Greenland concluded.

The following day, Szymon booked a flight to Rome. A couple of days later, he departed from San Francisco on American Airlines. After a long flight, he arrived at Leonardo da Vinci–Fiumicino Airport. Suffering from jet lag, he promptly went to bed after taking a taxi to Albani Hotel. The next day, he called the administrator of the American Overseas School of Rome and arranged for an interview with Palmira Goodman at 3:00 p.m. Szymon prepared diligently for the interview and even brought his black briefcase, wanting to appear professional. When Palmira entered the room, Szymon was captivated by her beauty.

She was a tall, slender woman with long blonde hair and stunning dark-brown eyes. Szymon believed that the eyes reflected the soul, and from the moment he saw hers, he was enchanted. After a brief introduction, he suggested that Palmira show him around the city she's been living in for the past ten years.

"As you know, my name is Szymon Tymor," he reintroduced himself.

"That's an unusual name," Palmira commented.

"And your name, Palmira, is quite unique as well."

"My mother loved palm trees."

"Ah, I see. I work as a journalist for the *Sentinel*, a newspaper in San Francisco. My boss sent me here to interview you."

"Why?"

"I suppose your family in Palo Alto is quite famous, and people in California would like to know what happened to your family after you left and how your life has been in Rome. Were you happy here during these last ten years?"

"Well, I was just a child when my mother and I came to Rome. I quickly learned Italian and tried to immerse myself in Italian culture as much as possible. It hasn't always been easy for me, though. My mother became ill about three years ago, and my life turned into a nightmare."

"I'm sorry to hear that."

"She passed away last month from pancreatic cancer."

"Do you think she could've been helped if she had stayed in California?"

"I don't think so. The Italian doctors said her cancer was inoperable, even in the United States. There was no hope for her."

"And your father, Dr. Goodman?"

"I don't know where he is. He disappeared. Some people say he committed suicide, but his body was never found. It's a real mystery. I loved my father dearly, and I miss him a lot."

"I heard that you want to study at Stanford. Is that true?"

"Yes, I want to return to California. I remember it always being so beautiful. In a few weeks, I'll be flying back home, and I hope to find out what happened to my father."

"If you don't mind, I'll help you search for him when we return to California. Since I'm a journalist, I know many people who can assist us. I'm quite familiar with the California investigation system. By the way, do you have a photo of your father?"

"Yes, I do. It's a photo of the two of us when I was nine."

"Please give it to me."

"It's at my apartment. I'll bring it tomorrow. By the way, if you'd like to see Rome, I'd be happy to show you around and be your tour guide."

"I gladly accept your offer. Thank you."

"How long will you be staying in Rome?"

"At least a week."

"I'm delighted to see a fellow American here in Rome."

"I'm certainly not an American in Paris."

"Then I'll see you tomorrow at 8:00 a.m. sharp in the lobby of your hotel."

The following morning, Palmira waited for Szymon in the Albani Hotel lobby. He noticed an old *New York Times* newspaper on one of the tables in the lobby. It dated back to 1975, and the headline read, "South Vietnam Invaded by North Vietnam."

"So much war," Szymon commented. "Isn't peace better? I recall the words of a wise and influential man who once said, 'People should and must erase wars from their history before wars erase all people from history.'"

"Amen. That's the truth," Palmira agreed. "Now let's go see the eternal city of Rome!"

Palmira hailed a cab from the taxi stand. They negotiated paying for the fare in dollars. Their cabdriver was a middle-aged man named Antonio. He was happy to show an American around town and talked continuously about his cousin living in New York.

They started their day at the main tourist attraction, the Colosseum, a large amphitheater that once housed sixty-five thousand spectators in the times of Ancient Rome. Szymon was so excited to see the Colosseum that he left his water bottle behind while taking photos.

Next, they visited the Pantheon, which was given to the Pope by Emperor Hadrian* in the year 608.

"This is the best-maintained building left from the Roman times. It has some unique monuments from Raphael, and a few kings are even buried here," Palmira explained.

Following the Pantheon, Palmira took Szymon to St. Peter's Basilica, which is the spiritual center of the Catholic church and the residence of the Pope. It's located in the independent state of Vatican City.

When they got inside St Peter's after waiting outside for over an hour in a very long line, Szymon's first stop was Michelangelo's masterpiece La Pietà.*

After visiting the crypts that housed the tombs of Popes throughout history, Szymon made a comment that in all these years, there was never a Polish Pope. He found this odd since Poland was a Christian country with a Jewish minority for a thousand years. Next, they visited the famous Sistine Chapel and admired countless Renaissance and Baroque masterpieces.

They left the Vatican and looked around for Antonio, who was waiting to drive them to the Trevi Fountain. The baroque fountain was built in the eighteenth century and features the god of the sea, Neptune*, on his chariot. Palmira thanked Antonio for his services and said they would walk the rest of the way.

"If you toss a coin into the Trevi Fountain, you'll be lucky enough to return to Rome someday," Palmira explained.

Szymon pulled a quarter out of his pocket and threw it in the fountain. After the Trevi Fountain, they walked to the Spanish Steps, in the Piazza di Spagna, and admired a much smaller fountain at the base of the steps.

Next, they walked to the Villa Borghese gardens, the most beautiful park in Rome, and admired the works of Rubens*, Bernini*, Caravaggio*, and Leonardo da Vinci.*

After the gardens, they strolled leisurely through Trastevere and noticed the Adriano movie theater featuring an old American film, *The Tender Trap*, starring Debbie Reynolds and Frank Sinatra.

"Looks like they only play old American movies at this theater. Would you like to see this one? It's a comedy set in New York, with a simple yet hilarious plot," Szymon asked Palmira.

"Why not? We have plenty of time," she replied.

They thoroughly enjoyed the movie, and Szymon couldn't resist whistling the catchy melody from the film as they exited the theater. The story revolved around three women in New York City attempting to ensnare an actor, portrayed by Frank Sinatra, into marriage. Szymon mentioned that he had memorized all the words of the title song when he watched the movie back home in San Francisco. Not content with just whistling, he began singing "(Love Is) The Tender Trap," with music by Jimmy Van Heusen and lyrics by Sammy Cahn. Imitating the great Frank Sinatra as they walked, he sang,

> You see a pair of laughing eyes,
> And suddenly you're sighing sighs
> You think nothing's wrong
> You string along, boy, then snap

Szymon snapped his fingers and continued singing, "La, la, la, la, la."

> Those eyes, those sighs,
> They're part of the tender trap
> Some starry night,
> When her kisses make you tingle,
> She'll hold you tight,
> And you'll hate yourself for being single
> And all at once, it seems so nice
> The folks are throwing shoes and rice
> You hurry to a spot that's just a dot on the map,
> And then you wonder how it all came about

Once again he snapped his fingers and sang, "La, la, la, la, la."

> It's too late now, there's no getting out,
> You fall in love, and love is a tender trap

Palmira applauded when Szymon finished singing. They were feeling thirsty and decided to stop at a bar. As they waited for their drinks, Palmira reached into her pocket and unfolded an envelope.

"Oh my god! I completely forgot to tell you about our plans for tomorrow. I got two tickets to the opera. Guess who will be singing the part of Arrigo in Giuseppe Verdi's opera *The Sicilian Vespers*?" she exclaimed.

"Who?" Szymon asked, curious.

"None other than Alberto Santini. He's been receiving fantastic reviews lately for his performances. Will you go with me to see this opera?" she asked.

"How could I refuse? Not in a million years. Of course, I'll join you," Szymon replied.

Palmira looked at Szymon, a little surprised that he accepted her invitation so readily. After enjoying a couple of drinks and sharing a delicious plate of pasta, she called a taxi and dropped Szymon off at his hotel.

"See you tomorrow at 7:00 p.m.," Palmira said, leaving the hotel.

Szymon was deeply impressed by Palmira and found himself developing a little crush on her. He desperately wanted to reach over and kiss her before she left but knew it wouldn't be appropriate.

The next evening, Palmira arrived at Szymon's hotel and waited for him in the lobby. She spotted him at the reception desk, handing his briefcase over to the concierge to lock in the hotel's safe.

"Sorry I'm late," he said.

"It's okay. You're only a few minutes late, and if we hurry, we'll still make it on time," Palmira replied.

They swiftly made their way to the Teatro dell'Opera di Roma to witness Alberto Santini's performance in Verdi's renowned opera.

Four hours later, Palmira and Szymon walked out of the opera house feeling electrified by the experience.

"*Fantastico!* Wasn't it great?" Palmira exclaimed.

"I'm sure my father would argue that the famous Polish opera singer Jan Kiepura* would have sung it even better. He was a devoted fan," Szymon said.

"You know, Szymon, Alberto Santini wants to fund my studies at Stanford," she mentioned.

"That's great, especially in your father's absence," he replied.

"You know, for some reason, I feel like my dad is still alive. Some days I feel like he's never left my side," Palmira said.

They found a taxi, and Palmira suggested stopping by her place.

"I would like to talk to you about California and my move there. Please come in," she said.

They entered Palmira's apartment. Szymon looked around and found the place cozy.

"Tell me about your parents, Szymon," Palmira initiated.

"There isn't much to say. My father was Polish, and my mom is Jewish. That's why I can speak both Polish and Yiddish fluently," he replied.

"So are you Jewish?" she asked.

"I was raised Catholic after my father, but I'm still half Jewish," he answered.

"So am I," she revealed.

"Really?" Szymon asked, surprised.

"You're a journalist, so you must enjoy writing," she stated.

"I prefer writing poetry," he responded.

"Poetry doesn't sell," she remarked.

"I know, but poetry runs in my blood. I caught the poetry bug from my mother," he replied.

"Is it challenging to be a good writer?" she inquired.

"Not really. You need ideas to write, but you also need a keen observation of people and the world around you," Szymon explained.

"What's the deal with that black briefcase you're always carrying around? Is it to hold money?" Palmira asked.

"It's a long story. One day, while my mother was searching for a book at the library, she stumbled upon an extraordinary poetry collection titled *Poetry from the Warsaw Ghetto*. It was published by a small company in Paris and written in Polish. Since I'm fluent in Polish, I translated two poems from that book into English. My mother told me to always keep these two poems with me because they were written in the Warsaw Ghetto by unknown authors. That's why I carry them in my briefcase. Most likely, these authors perished in the ghetto or died later in concentration camps. If you'd like to hear them, I can fetch my briefcase from the hotel. It shouldn't take me long. Just wait here. I'll be right back," Szymon said and left Palmira's apartment.

Szymon's hotel was nearby. After retrieving his briefcase, he hurried back to Palmira's apartment, so excited to read something to her that was so meaningful to him. Palmira sat comfortably in her chair, eagerly waiting as Szymon took out the first poem, titled "Jacob's Last Concerto," from his briefcase and began to read.

> There was an old Jacob playing the old fiddle,
> In the Warsaw Ghetto, standing in the middle.
> He was quiet, sad, and lost like a stone that cares,
> The war took his family—his wife, sons, and
> daughters.

He was like an oak, free eaten by cockroaches,
With cutoff branches and burned by torches.
A naked trunk, he knew what the wind is saying,
Crying for his lost kids in Yiddish, he starts praying.

Then he stood up and put the fiddle on his arm,
He started playing sadly with a certain charm.
He played steadily and softly, thinking of his son,
Who lost his life in darkness, not to see the sun.

Suddenly the strings began to wave like the sea,
Later you could hear the sounds as high as the tree.
Then silence! All frightened children joined hand
     in hand,
Everywhere they looked seemed strange: the blue
     sky, the land.

And only their lonely Jewish souls were praying,
They couldn't understand what Jacob was saying.
He played steadily, seems his music never lingers,
It looked like the tears were playing on his fingers.

Here in Warsaw, they were happy but died from
     a gun,
Glory of their race was sung from father to son.
What have we done so wrong? What have our
     lips said?
Did we deserve this moment to be right and dead?

To be burned and gassed alive while taking a bath?
Why did thousands of Davids lose to one Goliath?
Today they love the trees, the wind, the morning
     dew,
Tomorrow angry Nazis will shout, "Kill a Jew!"

Fate made us all equal with our strength and wit,
These in gold and rags and those in roses and shit.
Oh, Yahweh! Where are you? Tell me, whom you
          can trust?
If you exist, come down from Mount Sinai to us.

Help us! We are like the lost oars thrown overboard,
And like melting white snow touched by a magic
          sword.
Then Jacob calms the strings, untangles the sorrow,
Of uncertain today, uncertain tomorrow.

It seemed like he stopped, but no, he's changing
          the mood,
He's still a master, like a gull over a flood.
He's raising up his fiddle, searching for a dream,
With tears, he sings in Yiddish "El Malei
          Rachamim."

Then silence! Frightened, Jacob falls into despair,
Everybody's awakened; fright is in the air.
But no! He chokes his sadness, fright, despair,
          and tears,
Turning to strange uniforms full of fun and mirth.

Next, Jacob wants to leave all his friends forever,
His tones are cold, so deep, but fearful as never.
He's gathering all black clouds floating in the sky,
And, with lightning, strikes all men who don't
          weep or cry.

"You looked at the cities, the cities are burning,
Everything you touch turns to ashes and yearning.
Suffering will be worshiped by the next generation,
Time will reward us in fruits for our frustration.

Look up! This cloud above us is made from our
    blood,
And there is a hidden lightning by which you'll
    be struck."
Saying this, he gently touched the strings like his
    hair,
And suddenly a loud triumphant song was heard.

He played, he played so gently, so sad and so smart,
But he could not end…
An angry Nazi soldier shot him in the heart.

Jacob spread his arms out and fell on the fiddle,
Frightened people scattered; he lay in the middle.
Standing quietly and praying for Jacob from Shiloh,
Proud, brave people started to sing "Hava Nagila."

The day was beautiful. It was Easter Sunday,
Everyone felt so tense, preparing for Monday.
The day of the Jews' revolt in the Warsaw Ghetto,
Its beginning was Jacob's last concerto.

"This poem was beautiful, so very touching," Palmira commented.

When Szymon finished reading, Palmira took his hand and held it for a while, wanting him to feel supported. Szymon looked quietly out her window, at another beautiful Italian monument. As he pondered the poem he just recited, he decided that despite his Catholic upbringing, he wanted to commit to the Jewish faith when he returned home. He also made a promise to himself to help Palmira find her father.

"El Malei Rachamim," he said, almost sounding like he was crying.

"What is the meaning of this?" Palmira asked.

"It's a Hebrew prayer for the souls of lost heroes," he explained.

"Will you read me the other poem?" she asked.

"This other poem was also written by an unknown author from the Warsaw Ghetto. It's about a mother," he said. He started reciting it with a slight tremble in his voice.

> There's a grave of my mother in a cold, faraway
>   place,
> My golden Jewish mother, who knew all exciting
>   ways,
> An angry fascist killed her because she showed
>   me her love,
> He killed her in cold blood, having the heaven
>   above.
> Killing her, he killed a myth her goodness and
>   goodwill,
> When her body touched the pavement, there was
>   nothing more to kill.
> She left the field of glory without diamonds or
>   ambers,
> People might forget her, but the pavement…still
>   remembers.

When Szymon finished reading the poem, Palmira sat quietly, deep in her thoughts.

"It's hard to imagine how the author must have felt writing this," he said.

"You must really love your mother, don't you?" she asked.

"Yes, I do. I remember returning home from school with football trophies, and she'd put her hand on my head and call me her handsome Ashkenazim. So now you know what I carry in my black briefcase. My mother always wants me to remember my Jewish heritage," he replied.

"You know, Szymon, when we met, I really started thinking about my future. What's my destiny when I return to California? I had such a peaceful life here in Rome, but now I'm kind of scared. Will I find my father? I think of him all the time, wondering where he might be. Is he safe? Is he in danger? I'm bombarded by these frightening thoughts day and night," she said.

"Well, fate is like a waiter who sometimes might be late with service, so I'm not really concerned," he replied.

"Did you ever visit Israel, Szymon?" Palmira asked.

"Not yet. I haven't had the chance, but I know so much about the country and its people. You know, Israel began in Poland," he replied.

"Really?"

"Well, Israel's first two prime ministers were born in Poland, and more will likely follow. David Ben-Gurion was born David Grun in Płońsk, Poland. He was the first. Next was Shimon Peres, born Szymon Perski in Vishnyeva, Poland, now Belarus. He's my namesake. I could go on and on. There would have been no State of Israel without Jews who had lived in Poland for a thousand years. The city of Kraków was called the Polish Jerusalem, the city of Lublin was known as the Land of Israel, and the city of Łódź was called the Promised Land. But let's talk about something else. I saw some advertisements in my hotel about the Italian Riviera. Next time we're both here, maybe we can visit Portofino or San Remo?" he asked after his long speech.

"Maybe next time," she replied.

"So let me know your itinerary for California. I'd be happy to meet you at the airport when you arrive," he said.

They said their goodbyes, he kissed her on the cheek, and they parted ways.

THE TRIAL

ON AN EARLY SEPTEMBER DAY in 1977, a Pan Am Airlines flight from Rome landed at San Francisco International Airport with Szymon Tymor on board. He was happy to be back home in California. He was very tired and took a cab straight to his mother Sabina's apartment. He was living with her temporarily after his father died but planned to move as soon as he found a suitable apartment.

The next morning, his mother knocked on his bedroom door; and when nobody answered, she just walked in. Szymon was still sleeping from the jet lag. She stood over him for a while, watching him sleep, but finally decided to wake him up.

"Szymon, Mr. Greenland called and said that he is expecting you in his office," she said.

"I'm coming, I'm coming," Szymon grumbled.

"You know what? You should find yourself a nice girl and get married," Szymon's mother said.

"Knowing you, it would have to be a nice Jewish girl," he replied.

"Possibly," she said.

Although Szymon was still looking for an apartment, it seemed like he was never in a rush to find one. He had the best of both worlds; he was saving money by not paying rent, and his best friend, his mother, took care of him. Sabina loved Szymon so much. She was always at his service, making him coffee and breakfast every morning. Where else could he find a better arrangement?

Szymon wasn't thinking about making any serious commitments. He was still dating Cheryl Walker, but marriage was not on his mind.

He quickly got up, took a shower, grabbed a cup of coffee, and ran to the office. His boss, Pat Greenland, welcomed him with open arms.

"How was Italy, Szymon?" he asked.

"Great," Szymon replied.

"What about Italian culture?"

"It's still there," Szymon joked.

"Did you get to see the Italian Riviera?" Pat inquired.

"Not enough time. Maybe next time," Szymon replied.

"And the history?" Pat asked.

"I took in so much history, especially regarding the Catholic Church," Szymon said.

During his visit, Szymon was taught about the abundant history of Catholicism in Rome, but he was also surprised to learn so much about Europe's Judeo-Christian roots. Szymon reached for his briefcase and took out the notebook that contained the interview with Palmira Goodman. He handed Pat the notebook.

"So how is Palmira Goodman?" he asked.

"She is a beautiful and smart young woman. She misses California. I will be meeting her at the airport next week" Szymon said.

"I see. It looks like you two really hit it off," Greenland said.

"You were right when you said that she wants to study at Stanford. Alberto Santini is going to pay her tuition. We met him at Rome's Opera Theatre, singing in Verdi's 'The Sicilian Vespers.' He has a great voice," Szymon told Greenland.

"And Palmira's mother?" Pat asked.

"She died last year of pancreatic cancer," Szymon replied.

"I'm sorry to hear that. Did Palmira hear anything new about her father?" Pat asked.

"She just knows what we all know. He disappeared. I promised to help her to look for him when she's back in California," he replied.

Szymon was very happy to be back at the office. Before he left for Rome, his coworkers were constantly bothering him with questions about Reverse Polish Notation (RPN). They needed some help with their Texas Instruments calculators and were sure that since he was Polish, Szymon could give them some tips about RPN. He didn't know too much about it because he wasn't a mathematician or an engineer, just a journalist. However, he once worked on an article about Silicon Valley and met a Polish computer engineer named Jerzy, so he connected his coworkers to him so they could learn more about RPN directly from an expert.

When Szymon got home, his mother gave him a message from Cheryl Walker. He returned Cheryl's call and was invited to attend her sister's birthday party at her parents' house. He still remembered the New Year's Eve party and Cheryl's father, John Walker. Szymon decided to attend the party.

Cheryl greeted him warmly but seemed a bit agitated. Szymon told her about his trip to Rome, but he omitted the part about meeting Palmira. He simply mentioned that his boss, Pat Greenland, sent him to Rome to learn more about Italian culture for an upcoming article at the *Sentinel*.

"So, Szymon, how was your trip to Rome?" she asked coldly.

"It was okay. I saw a lot of amazing things, but I'm glad to be back," he replied.

"Did you see the Pope?" she asked.

"No, but I visited Saint Peter's Basilica in Vatican City," Szymon said.

"I'm already jealous. Listen, I've been thinking. Can you tell me? Do you think we could ever be together?" she asked. Cheryl took out a cigarette and lit it.

Szymon put his arm around her and watched her smoke without saying anything. "What do you mean by *together*? Together in bed? Together as a couple?" Are we meant to be together in marriage?" he asked, his voice filled with uncertainty.

"When I say *together*, I mean close to you forever," she replied, her tone gentle and sincere.

"Nonsense! Women only think about the present, the here and now. Men think about the future. We have plans. Women see tomorrow as a dull day with the same man," Szymon asserted.

"That's only because men lack imagination," Cheryl responded with a hint of sarcasm.

"That's not true. It's because you're not loyal to your own feelings," Szymon countered.

"The struggle for lasting emotional connection is an eternal battle for women," Cheryl stated, her expression now more serious.

The debate continued back and forth until Szymon decided to put an end to it. "Enough of this pointless discussion. We won't change each other's minds," he declared.

"Would you like to kiss me for a change?" she inquired, breaking the tension.

"I'd rather you kiss me," he playfully retorted.

She smiled, leaned in, and placed a gentle kiss on his cheek. "Are you happy?" she whispered.

"Happiness is a complex concept, Cheryl," he replied thoughtfully.

"You're a remarkable man, Szymon. I could love you, but I'm afraid," she confessed. She wrapped her arms around his neck, pulling his face closer to hers, but he refrained from kissing her.

"You smell nice," he commented.

"It's my perfume," she responded.

Szymon observed Cheryl's peculiar behavior, realizing how needy she had become since he left for Rome. He couldn't help but reminisce about the free-spirited, fun-loving girl she used to be. Now it seemed like her only goal was to find a potential husband. Szymon knew they had a physical connection, but he had a difficult time feeling any real affection toward her. He yearned for a deeper connection with someone that he could truly commit to. Meeting Palmira convinced him that that he could someday find true love. He was consumed by thoughts of her.

Szymon grew weary of Cheryl's incessant talk about her esteemed family and decided it was time to leave the party. He grabbed his coat and bid his farewells.

As promised, on the day Palmira was meant to arrive in San Francisco, Szymon was there to greet her. Spotting Palmira among the passengers exiting the TWA terminal, he surprised her with a grand bouquet of roses. Palmira's nervousness about whether Szymon would be there to welcome her quickly dissipated. Also at the airport was Paula Niekro, the housekeeper from the Goodmans' Palo Alto residence. Paula had been corresponding with Palmira through letters and kindly offered her the use of an apartment in Palo Alto until she found her own place.

After a brief introduction, Paula provided Szymon with her home address and phone number and keys to the apartment. Observing Szymon's amiable relationship with Palmira, she trusted that he would take good care of her.

A week had passed since Palmira's arrival in California, yet Szymon had still not contacted her. He understood she needed to rest after such a tiring journey. Furthermore, he was occupied with something concerning Palmira's father. He had taken the photo Palmira gave him and made multiple copies. Throughout the week, he visited every police station in San Francisco and distributed the copies. When he left the last police station, he realized how willing he was to do whatever it took to bring Palmira happiness.

Szymon wasted no time. The following week, he called Palmira and invited her to join him for a tour of San Francisco since she hadn't seen the city in over ten years. Delighted to see Szymon and eager to explore some old, familiar places, Palmira happily accepted the invitation.

Szymon arrived at Paula's apartment and patiently waited in his car. Within minutes Palmira hopped into the car, ready for an adventure. Szymon began driving toward downtown when Palmira suddenly interrupted.

"Szymon, could we go to Palo Alto first? I'd like to visit my childhood home," she requested, her voice filled with nostalgia.

"Of course, Palmira. Your wish is my command," he replied, laughing.

As they drove toward Palo Alto, Palmira recognized her childhood home from a distance. Tears welled up in her eyes as she reminisced about her once-happy childhood when both of her parents were alive. Now her mother was dead, and her father had vanished. Because his body had never been found, she always kept her father's memory close to her heart and prayed for his safe return someday. Noticing her grief, Szymon suggested they take a little break from going down memory lane.

"How about I show you around San Francisco, the city you likely don't remember too much of? Would that be all right?" he proposed.

"Of course! I would love to see it," she responded with enthusiasm.

First, they stopped at the Hilton hotel for lunch. Szymon's resourcefulness swiftly secured them a table, and Palmira was impressed. In no time, they were seated and waiting for their drinks. Szymon initiated the conversation.

"You know, Palmira, when I was a little boy still living in Poland, I had a friend named Bartek. But Bartek wasn't a human friend. He was a bird, a white stork," Szymon began, a nostalgic smile gracing his face. "Storks migrate to Poland and other European countries from as far away as Africa. In early spring, I would eagerly await Bartek's return. For three consecutive years, Bartek nested on the roof of my parents' house. During that time, Bartek and his partner produced twelve offspring, twelve adorable baby storks. The first year, there were three. The second year, four. And in the third year, five. Can you imagine? I loved each one of them. White storks are incredibly graceful birds with black wing tips, reddish beaks, and slender legs. They come to Poland to breed and enjoy the plentiful food supply. They thrive on frogs, which can be found in Polish lakes, marshes, and swamps. By the end of August or early September, they embark on their return journey to Africa," Szymon concluded.

"It seems like you had a wonderful childhood, Szymon," Palmira remarked, touched by his story.

At that moment, Szymon noticed a gray-haired man accompanied by a young blonde leaving the restaurant. He leaned in closer to Palmira and whispered in her ear.

"Do you see that older man leaving with the young blonde?" he asked, his voice lowered.

"Yes," Palmira replied, her gaze fixed on the departing couple.

"I know him. His name is Tews. I once wrote a poem about him. Would you like to hear it? I'm sure you remember my fondness for poetry from our time together in Rome?" he inquired.

"All right, go ahead," Palmira agreed, wanting to please him.

Szymon began reciting his poem with gusto.

> Mr. Tews hates all Jews without any reason,
> A pious anger turns inside him from season to
> season.
> But whenever a rich Jew puts money in his case,
> He constantly reminds him how good and pure
> is the Jewish race.

"Well, did you like it?" Szymon asked, awaiting Palmira's response.

"You and your poetry! Perhaps you should write more poetry," Palmira teased with a smile on her lips.

"I am a journalist, so I write regardless," he replied with a chuckle.

"You mentioned in Rome that you enjoy poetry because of your mom," Palmira reminisced, recalling their previous conversation.

"Palmira, I wanted to let you know that I distributed copies of your father's picture to many police stations across San Francisco," he informed her.

"Thank you," she replied gratefully, planting a gentle kiss on his lips. As she did, Szymon's affection for Palmira grew even stronger. He realized that she was becoming an integral part of his future, and he was slowly falling in love with her.

"Palmira, are you ready to attend Stanford University?" Szymon inquired, his curiosity piqued.

"Yes, I am. I believe my dad would be proud of me," she responded, her voice tinged with a mix of excitement and longing.

"There's something else I want to share with you. I've been searching for an apartment as well. I'm planning to move out of my mother's place. It's been long overdue for me to have my own space, and I think she's also ready to live independently now," he explained.

"Your mother, Sabina, the one who enjoys poetry?" Palmira confirmed.

"Yes, the very same. In fact, when I got back from Rome, I purchased a condo in one of those high-rise buildings in the city. It was a great deal. The condo is situated on the forty-fourth floor, offering breathtaking views," Szymon shared, a sense of pride evident in his voice.

"I'm so proud of you, Szymon. How spacious is the place?" Palmira inquired.

"It's not overly spacious, but it's comfortable. It features a bedroom, a kitchen, a bathroom, and a small den. You might think it's a paradise with all the amenities, but the truth is it's a bit of a mess," Szymon confessed, a touch of amusement in his tone.

"Oh, really? What's going on?" Palmira asked, intrigued by his description.

"Picture this. Whenever I turn on the faucet in the kitchen, the lights start flickering. And when I turn the lights off, the water in the sink backs up. Then when I turn the lights on again, some strange fumes emanate from the fan. Not in my condo, mind you, but in my neighbor's place on the forty-fifth floor. Whenever my neighbor turns off the gas on his stove, my lights go out. The heater isn't any better. When it's turned on, the freezer in the refrigerator stops working. The list goes on," Szymon concluded, a mischievous smile playing on his lips.

Palmira burst into laughter. "I can never be sure if you're being serious or if this is another one of your poetic tales," she remarked, thoroughly entertained.

"Oh, this time I'm very serious. After noticing all these issues, I considered just selling the condo before even moving in," Szymon admitted, hoping she would understand his predicament.

Szymon escorted Palmira back to Paula Niekro's apartment, and they exchanged affectionate goodbyes. He assured her that he would be in touch as soon as possible.

The following day, while lighting a cigarette in his office, Pat Greenland inquired about Szymon's future.

"What are your plans, Szymon? Do you intend to get married and settle down?" Pat asked, genuinely curious.

"Perhaps someday, sir. I'm in no rush," Szymon replied, contemplating his future.

"What about Palmira Goodman? She's back in California, and you seem to really like her," Pat probed, his interest evident.

"I hope she'd be interested in dating me, but at the moment, I'm focused on helping in her quest to find her father," Szymon revealed.

"I know that marriage is considered outdated these days, but I must admit I'm a happily married man even though I occasionally clash with my mother-in-law. She's a wonderful woman, though," Pat shared, chuckling softly.

"Speaking of mothers-in-law, a Jewish joke comes to mind. 'Why did Adam from the Garden of Eden live so long? Because he had no mother-in-law,'" Szymon quipped.

"We can laugh and joke, but Jewish mothers-in-law are the best. And they're phenomenal cooks!" Pat added, sharing his own perspective.

"In all honesty, most women are smarter than men," Szymon remarked thoughtfully.

"Have you found any Californian women intriguing?" Pat inquired, genuinely interested in his perspective.

"Undoubtedly, many of them are. However, I know one girl in San Francisco who only cares about fast cars, fun, and money. It doesn't matter whom she chooses as her boyfriend or lover as long as he owns a Jaguar and has deep pockets," Szymon responded poetically.

"You and your poetry, Szymon. Please go on," Pat encouraged him.

"All right, then. When I informed her that I'm a man of many words, I love books, and I have my own unique worldview, she went around telling her friends that I was foolish," Szymon recounted.

"And since you mentioned poetry, there's a wonderful poem by a well-known Polish poet, Julian Tuwim, titled 'ABC of a Gossip Abecadło.' I even translated it into English because I found it incredibly amusing."

"I hope it's a good one," Pat remarked.

"Well, you can judge for yourself," Szymon replied and proceeded to recite Tuwim's poem.

Once, Count C and Baron Z
Walked leisurely toward the open sea.
The count divulged a secret gossip:
"Did you know that Marquess L
And Lady H had an affair in the heady green dell?
It's a delightful folly, I must say.

Baron Z, seething with anger,
Met two gentlemen, R and F,
And casually mentioned,
"Do you know that Lady B and Major O
Read the *Kama Sutra* and became pros?
It's a scandalous sensation in town."

This entire ABC, what a pity,
Like a thunderclap, it struck the city.
A parasitic tapeworm was born,
Feeding on those mysterious letters.

Who heard about it? Actor E,
Who proclaimed, "This count is nothing but a
    big a———."
Thus, gossip spread throughout the town,
In abundance and galore.

That Duchess A is a common wh———
And that Prince J has a child with her,
It's all a big lie, believe me, sir.

And here comes S, I only know,
That Lady G lives with big, bad M with stinky feet,
But M is simply full of shit.
He stole from O and E and L,
And R with K entrusted me,
With secret information.

And wild muddle started quick,
E reviled L, U beat up Z,
They sent letters to the papers,
Be quiet, S, L, and E,
It's her concern and hers alone,
And L and P are boors, no less.

In this place, it's great to be,
This whole alphabet, ABC.
And here ended the fetters
Of those secreted letters.

Szymon finished reciting the poem, awaiting Pat's reaction.

"Gossip truly has a way of spreading like wildfire. Thanks for sharing, Szymon," Pat said, enjoying the lighthearted moment.

Meanwhile, as Szymon and Mr. Greenland were engaging in their conversation, Hector Morales was working in San Jose at his thriving bakery, largely because of the growing popularity of Dr. Juan. Dr. Juan was gaining recognition for providing not only medical advice but also homeopathic treatments, leading many to stop seeing Dr. Fernando Sanchez at the local clinic.

One of Dr. Juan's patients, Mr. Flores, sought treatment for stomach pain. Suspecting he had stomach ulcers, Dr. Juan recommended he drink an herbal tea of dried *Achillea millefolium* (yarrow) leaves, known for their potential to ease pain and heal ulcers. Legend has it that the plant was named after Achilles, the Greek mythical hero, who used it to stop his soldiers' wounds from bleeding.

Mr. Flores mentioned this treatment to Dr. Sanchez during a visit to his clinic, which greatly upset Dr. Sanchez.

Dr. Sanchez angrily confronted Dr. Juan at the bakery, "Are you this quack, Dr. Juan?"

Dr. Juan calmly replied, "Yes, and I'm helping people who have no insurance and little money."

Dr. Sanchez was visibly frustrated and accused him of practicing without a medical license. He even threatened Dr. Juan with legal consequences.

"You want me to go prison? For helping people?" Dr. Juan questioned, perplexed.

Not taking the matter lightly, Dr. Sanchez followed through on his threat and filed a lawsuit against Dr. Juan at the Hall of Justice court in San Jose.

Back in San Francisco, Szymon was meeting his best friend, Mark Meihsner, for lunch at the Hilton hotel. Despite Mark's tardiness, they were very enthusiastic about their reunion.

"Sorry I'm late. This damn traffic is getting worse every year!" Mark apologized. He was thrilled to see Szymon after such a long time apart.

"You mentioned having something important to tell me. What's on your mind?" Szymon inquired, eager for the conversation to unfold.

"Well, let me begin. I have fantastic news. I've been selected as a public defender in a lawsuit filed by Dr. Fernando Sanchez against Dr. Juan, also known as Juan Alvarez, at the courthouse in San Jose. Dr. Sanchez is accusing Dr. Juan of being a charlatan. It's a fascinating case!" Mark exclaimed.

The trial was scheduled for October 16, 1977. On that day, lawyers, paralegals, and medical experts gathered at Hall of Justice court, filling the courtroom with anticipation. As Judge William Brown entered the room, the atmosphere grew even more charged. The proceedings commenced with Edward Cannon, the prosecuting attorney, calling Hector Morales to the witness stand. Hector took an oath, vowing to tell the truth, and settled into the witness stand.

Prosecutor Cannon addressed Hector. "Mr. Morales, is it true that ten years ago, you found the accused Dr. Juan on the road, left for dead?"

Hector replied, "Yes, sir. My son Julio and I were driving from San Francisco to San Jose when we stumbled on Dr. Juan lying injured on the pavement. It appeared he had been robbed and thrown out of a car. We took him to the San Jose's Good Samaritan Hospital, where Dr. Johnson informed us that his injuries were more severe than anticipated. He developed amnesia from the head trauma and didn't even know his name or where he came from. After his release, I offered him a job at my bakery as well as a place to stay. We named him Juan Alvarez."

Prosecutor Cannon continued questioning Hector. "Mr. Morales, how did Juan Alvarez come to be known as Dr. Juan?"

Hector explained, "We began calling him Dr. Juan after he helped my son Julio with an old baseball injury. Then he started consulting with my uninsured customers and providing them with his homeopathic treatments."

Mark Meihsner, Dr. Juan's public defender, then called Dr. Fernando Sanchez to the witness stand.

Dr. Sanchez took an oath and stood as a witness for the prosecution.

Mark addressed Dr. Sanchez. "Dr. Sanchez, do you recall Julio Morales as your patient?"

Dr. Fernando Sanchez affirmed, "Yes, I do. He broke his arm playing baseball, and I performed the surgery."

Mark continued, "Was your surgery successful? Did you do everything necessary for Julio's full recovery?"

Dr. Sanchez defended himself, stating, "I thought I did until this charlatan, Dr. Juan, told Julio his bones were misaligned. Can you imagine? This Dr. Juan, who isn't even a surgeon, miraculously aligned his bones properly just by massaging Julio's hand. I couldn't believe my eyes when I saw the results."

Mark Meihsner then pressed the doctor, "Dr. Sanchez, if patients chose to see Dr. Juan instead of you, doesn't that indicate that they believed he could provide better care? Could it be that you filed this lawsuit out of jealousy?"

Dr. Sanchez retorted, "It's not about jealousy. The fact is Dr. Juan doesn't possess a medical license. I checked every medical school in the United States, and there's no record of a Juan Alvarez or Dr. Juan. He must be some sort of quack."

To shed light on Dr. Juan's condition, Mark Meihsner called Dr. Frank Johnson from San Jose's Good Samaritan Hospital to the witness stand. He inquired, "Dr. Johnson, from a medical perspective, is it possible for someone like Dr. Juan to experience memory loss from hitting their head against the pavement?"

Dr. Frank Johnson responded, "Absolutely. It's called retrograde amnesia. Cases of this nature were documented after World War II. Retrograde amnesia erases a person's previous life from their memory."

Amid the courtroom drama, Mark Meihsner called Dr. Juan himself to the witness stand. He questioned, "Dr. Juan, do you have a family?"

Dr. Juan replied, "No, I have nobody. The people I live and work with, like Hector Morales and his relatives, are my family. Hector helped me when I needed it most, offering me a place to live and work."

Mark Meihsner continued, "Did any of your Latino patients die?"

Dr. Juan confidently responded, "No, none. I'm extremely cautious and only provide natural remedies like herbs and plants to my patients."

Mark Meihsner remarked, "Even so, it's remarkable how much medical knowledge you possess."

Dr. Juan humbly replied, "I don't know how I learned so much about medicine. I can't remember."

Mark Meihsner then turned his attention to Prosecutor Cannon. "Obviously, we must address the issue of quackery and charlatanism in the state of California. However, let's not forget that Dr. Juan has been undeniably valuable to the people he's treated. He brings them relief and helps them regain a sense of purpose after healing their troubling ailments. He's essential to this community."

Suddenly Mark Meihsner had a strange intuition. All the hairs on his arms stood up. He pulled out a picture of Palmira's father that Szymon had given him and looked closely at Dr. Juan. The moment he realized it, he exclaimed, "Oh my god!" All eyes turned toward Mark as he rushed out of the courtroom and called Szymon from the hallway.

"Szymon, please come to San Jose's Hall of Justice court as soon as possible, and bring Palmira with you. We're in room number 2. Please hurry," Mark urgently requested.

Curious, Szymon asked, "Why the rush?"

"When I have suspicion, I'm often correct," Mark replied.

After waiting for three nerve-racking hours, Mark spotted Szymon and Palmira entering the courtroom where Dr. Juan's trial was taking place. As soon as Palmira caught sight of Dr. Juan, she ran toward him, tears streaming down her face, and embraced him. She cried out, "Daddy, Daddy, it's really you!"

Dr. Juan looked taken aback, and everyone in the room was equally confused. He embraced Palmira, uncertain of who she was because of his memory loss.

Palmira turned toward the judge and declared loudly, "My name is Palmira Goodman." Pointing at Dr. Juan, she continued, "And this is my father, Dr. Steven Goodman. I haven't seen him for ten years after my mother took me to live in Rome. The California media reported that he disappeared, and I feared he was dead. But I always believed that when I returned to California, I would find him. I prayed every day to see him again because I love him so much."

Her words seemed to jolt Dr. Juan out of his amnesia; memories started flooding back. The room was stunned into silence. Dr. Johnson approached Palmira and her father, embracing them both.

"I was certain that your father could regain his memory once he saw someone from his past, and you, Palmira, made it happen," Dr. Johnson exclaimed.

Dr. Steven Goodman held Palmira tightly; he might not have seen her for ten years, but he always carried her in his heart. A father's love never dies.

"I have so much to tell you, Palmira, about my life here and all the wonderful people who have helped me. Thanks to my job at Morales Bakery, I can even bake you some bread," Dr. Goodman said, his voice filled with emotion as he continued to hug his daughter.

Judge Brown concluded the trial with these final words: "This trial is unexpectedly and happily dismissed."

THE WEDDING

EVERYONE WAS STILL IN DISBELIEF that Dr. Juan was the missing surgeon from Stanford University Hospital. Because Steven Goodman had suffered such severe memory loss and Palmira was his only family member, Dr. Johnson suggested that she take her father to San Jose's Good Samaritan Hospital for more tests and observation.

An ambulance was called to transport Dr. Goodman to the hospital. Palmira promised her father that she would visit him every day to check on his progress. Both Palmira and her father had a lot to catch up on after ten years of separation.

At one of her visits, Palmira was joined by Szymon Tymor and Mark Meihsner. Palmira jokingly introduced Szymon as her future fiancé. On hearing the introduction, Szymon realized that it was time to take the next step in their relationship. He went to the Lang jewelry store in San Francisco, bought a large diamond engagement ring, and finally proposed to Palmira. He had known for a long time, even back in Rome, that he was in love with her and that Cheryl Walker was a thing of the past.

Palmira understood that it would take some time for her relationship with her father to normalize. After all, they had been separated for so long, and her father was still working on regaining his memory. Dr. Goodman also wanted to learn everything about Palmira and his former wife's lives in Rome. When Palmira mentioned Sharon's passing, she noticed tears welling up in her father's eyes. She held his hand and realized that he still loved Sharon despite her leaving him for another man.

Steven was overjoyed and proud to learn about Palmira's plans to attend Stanford University. "Do you want to study medicine?" he asked Palmira.

"No, Dad. I've been thinking about studying journalism or law, and Szymon has offered to support me," she replied.

"You are a very intelligent young woman, and I have faith in you," Dr. Goodman said.

Palmira, Szymon, and Mark remained in Dr. Goodman's room for hours, hanging on to every word. His memory was gradually returning, although it took some time. He could now recall how his wife, Sharon, had left him for the opera singer Alberto Santini, and he remembered receiving her letter confessing her betrayal. He even remembered being assaulted by robbers, thrown out of a car, and left to die on the road.

They listened intently as Dr. Goodman recounted his story of being found on the road and receiving help from a kind Latino family. He spoke of Hector Morales, who had given him a job at the Morales Bakery, where he worked hard to support himself. It was during this time that he became known as Dr. Juan, providing medical assistance to the local Latino community without accepting any payment.

In fact, many of his patients testified in his favor during the trial, serving as living examples of his medical skills as Dr. Juan, or, rather, Dr. Steven Goodman. When he finished his story, Palmira held her father's hand and expressed her sympathy for the suffering he had endured over the past ten years.

"My dear, let's leave these painful memories behind us and focus on the future," Dr. Goodman said, comforting her.

Palmira then asked about the possibility of reclaiming their house in Palo Alto. Dr. Goodman wasn't optimistic but assured her that he would try everything to make it happen. In the meantime, he was renting a small apartment in San Francisco.

*****

Szymon, wanting to check on Dr. Goodman's well-being in his new place, paid him a visit.

"Hello, Dr. Goodman. I'm glad to see you're feeling better," Szymon greeted him, glancing around the furnished apartment.

"The most important thing is that my memory is improving," Dr. Goodman replied.

"I like your new place. It's in a nice neighborhood and, most importantly, already furnished, saving you the hassle of buying furniture. On the other hand, I, the crazy Polack, bought a condominium that seems to have endless problems. Every time I fix one thing, another issue arises. But enough about that. I came here to discuss my and Palmira's future. Ever since I met Palmira in Rome, I knew I would marry her one day. I wasn't sure if I could convince her to stay in the United States, but her determination to find you brought her here. We're engaged now, and I wanted to ask if you would walk Palmira down the aisle at our wedding," Szymon asked.

"The wedding? So soon? Are you certain about your love for her?" Dr. Goodman inquired.

"I am absolutely certain, and she wouldn't have accepted the engagement ring if she didn't love me," Szymon affirmed.

"Of course, I will do it. She is my only daughter, and I wouldn't miss it for the world," Dr. Goodman agreed.

"Now I'm just not sure if Palmira will want to move into my condo with all the issues I've been having," Szymon added.

"If she loves you, she will be willing to live with you no matter how many problems you encounter at your condo." Dr. Goodman chuckled.

*****

Preparations for the wedding were underway. Palmira and Szymon decided to have a small ceremony at San Francisco's Ocean Beach with a small group of family and friends in attendance. Szymon's best friend, Mark, served as his best man. Dr. Goodman walked Palmira down the aisle to where Szymon eagerly awaited her.

Szymon's mother, Sabina, was overjoyed that her son had found love and that she no longer had to worry about his future.

Szymon watched every step Palmira took as she approached him at the altar. She looked radiant in her simple wedding dress, holding a small bouquet of lily of the valley. Though both Palmira and Szymon were only half Jewish, they had chosen to have a rabbi officiate their wedding. After exchanging their vows and sealing them with a kiss, they declared themselves Mr. and Mrs. Tymor to the roaring cheers of their loved ones.

Szymon held Palmira close and whispered, "You have no idea how beautiful you are. Of all the women I've ever met, none of them can compare to you. None possess your unique charm. I fell in love with you when we were in Rome. To me, every move, every smile, and every glance you make is a work of art."

Palmira replied, "You'll always be my favorite poet."

They celebrated with a small reception at a nearby restaurant, enjoying seafood and local wine from Napa Valley. They danced for a while; and as midnight approached, the party came to an end, marking the beginning of a new day.

It took time and effort, but Dr. Goodman eventually regained possession of his house. After a couple of months, he moved back in and returned to work at Stanford University Hospital. While he couldn't perform complex brain surgeries because of his lingering doubts, he was content to serve as a staff surgeon. As for Palmira and Szymon, they enjoyed their honeymoon in Hawaii and lived happily ever after.

So whatever happened to the renowned surgeon who later became known as the mystery healer? Well, he rose to prominence within California's Latino community, establishing himself as a revered and dependable physician. Patients sought his expertise from far and wide and benefited in numerous ways from his wise counsel and skilled care.

APPENDIX

Immanuel Kant—A German philosopher; the central figure in modern philosophy and one of the central Enlightenment thinkers. p. 22.

Frederic Chopin—A Polish composer and virtuoso pianist of the Romantic period. He wrote primarily for solo piano. He has maintained worldwide renown as a leading musician of his era. p. 22.

Felix Mendelssohn—A German composer, pianist, music conductor, and teacher. One of the most celebrated figures of the early Romantic period. p. 22.

Plock—A city in central Poland on the River Vistula located north of Warsaw. Several Polish kings are buried in the Plock cathedral. p. 22.

Baltic Sea—A semi-enclosed inland sea located in Northern Europe, connected to the Atlantic Ocean by the Danish Straits. p. 22.

Emperor Hadrian—A Roman emperor; One of the so-called Five Good Emperors. He is known for his travels throughout the empire and the civil and military constructions of his reign. p. 34.

La Pieta—One of Michelangelo's first major works. It is a marble sculpture of Jesus and Mary at Mount Golgotha representing the "sixth sorrow". p. 34.

Neptune—Roman god of waters and seas who controlled winds and storms. p. 35.

Peter Paul Rubens—A Flemish painter who was the greatest exponent of Baroque paintings with its dynamism, vitality, and sensuous exuberance. p. 35.

Gian Lorenzo Bernini—An Italian sculptor and architect credited with creating the Baroque style of sculpture. p. 35.

Caravaggio—Italian painter active in Rome f or most of his artistic life. His paintings are known for their intense realism. p. 35.

Leonardo da Vinci—The Renaissance genius who revolutionized art and science with his masterpieces like the Mona Lisa. He was a painter, engineer, architect, and inventor. He is among the most influential artists in history. p. 35.

Jan Kiepura—A Polish opera singer and actor in the twentieth century. p. 37.

ABOUT THE AUTHOR

HAVING A NICE VOICE, HE wanted to be a singer and desired to be on the stage, but he always wanted to be a writer of stories. Perry Dantes, aka Perry Nowakowski, was born in Aleksandrow Kujawski, Poland. He attended Nicolaus Copernicus University in Poland and the University of Wisconsin–Milwaukee.